THIS BOOK BELONGS TO

Losing Titus

by Cameron Pendergraft

Illustrated by Jennifer Tipton Cappoen

Text copyright 2022 by Cameron Pendergraft. Illustrations copyright 2022 by Jennifer Tipton Cappoen. All rights reserved. No part of this book may be reproduced or transmitted in any form or by any means, electronic or mechanical, including photography, recording, or any information storage and retrieval system, without permission in writing from the publisher. The only exceptions are brief excerpts and reviews.

Author: Cameron Pendergraft
Cover Designer and Illustrator: Jennifer Tipton Cappoen
Editor: Lynn Bemer Coble

PCKids is an imprint of **Paws and Claws Publishing, LLC.**
1589 Skeet Club Road, Suite 102 #175
High Point, NC 27265
www.PawsandClawsPublishing.com
info@pawsandclawspublishing.com

ISBN # 978-1-946198-32-7
Printed in the United States

Dedication
Dedicated to Jennifer, Scott, Hayes, and Tanner.
In memoriam of Titus.

Titus was the best dog. My mom would say
that to him again and again.
"You are the best dog, Titus."
Our family thought that he was.

Titus crossed the "Rainbow Bridge"
last month. Our family is still very sad.

Titus was the largest puppy in his litter.
And so, my dad thought the name
"Titus" suited him.
It did.

Titus loved a boat ride! He got excited when he saw our boat hitched to our truck. Titus raced to jump into the backseat before we had a chance to load our towels and cooler!

I knew something was wrong with Titus when he did not get excited the last time my dad hitched the boat for a trip to the lake. He didn't even try to get up when my dad blew the truck's horn.

Our home is in the country. Titus loved to hunt and to bring "prizes"—or gifts—to us. We called them his "prizes." He acted like they were!

He proudly dropped a mole that he had pulled out of the ground at our back door. We praised him as he pranced gallantly with a stinky, dead fish in his mouth.

Dad said that was Titus's way of showing us that he loved us.
I knew he did.

We all knew Titus loved us.

We loved him more.

Therefore, it has taken our family a very long time to say his name or to talk about him since he died.

Yes. Titus died. I don't like that word.
It sounds like the end.

I called Titus "TiTi." The first time he met me he was so curious to smell me that he poked me in my head with his nose. That made me cry.

When I got older, I taught Titus how to play hide-and-seek. I would hide and my dad would yell, "Go find Hayes!"

Titus loved cheese.
He sat and drooled when my dad fired up the grill for Cheeseburger Night.

We all knew something wasn't right when Titus lost interest in a cheeseburger.

Titus had a *huge* appetite! He would usually eat anything.

Marshmallows cooked over our backyard fire pit were always a hit with Titus. My brother, Tanner, knew the dog liked the burnt ones. He tossed those to Titus. The dog's teeth *chomped* as he jumped up and then gobbled each one with a gulp!

Recently our family tried to start a fire to roast marshmallows. We decided to wait a while.

It just wasn't the same without Titus.

My mother insisted on washing Titus's paws before he'd step inside our house. Oh, he *despised* that!

Mom said yesterday that if we could just have Titus back for one more day, she'd let his dirty paws pad all over our house.

Wouldn't that be something, to have Titus come back?

His first collar was orange. I found it the other day at the bottom of his toy basket.

Dad wants to hang on to that old basket "for a while," he says.

Titus could talk.
He tried to make sounds like words.

My dad could get him to ask for breakfast.
Those moans and grunts and howls of
Titus's sounded funny.

We always put a bandana on him for
pictures.
"You look so handsome," we insisted.

We buried Titus in his red bandana.
That was his favorite. Ours too.

My mom says that Titus followed her everywhere. She misses her shadow.

Titus loved it when we had folks get together at our house.

He knew lots of tricks and liked to show them off.

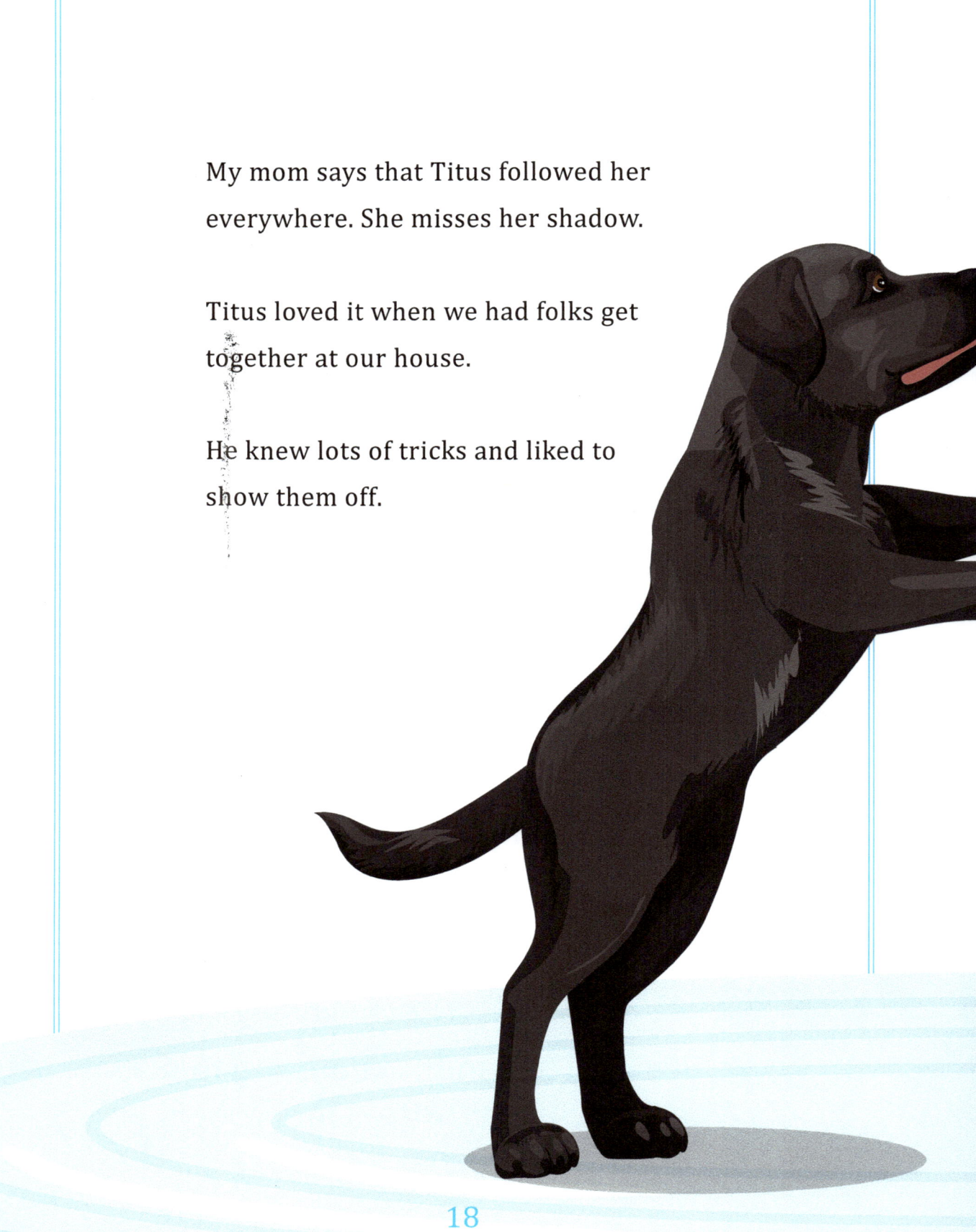

Titus had nicknames:
Boogie, Boogie-Woogie, Monte-Monte, to name a few.

Boogi

"Only the most special beings get nicknames," my papa always says.

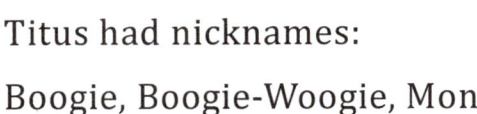

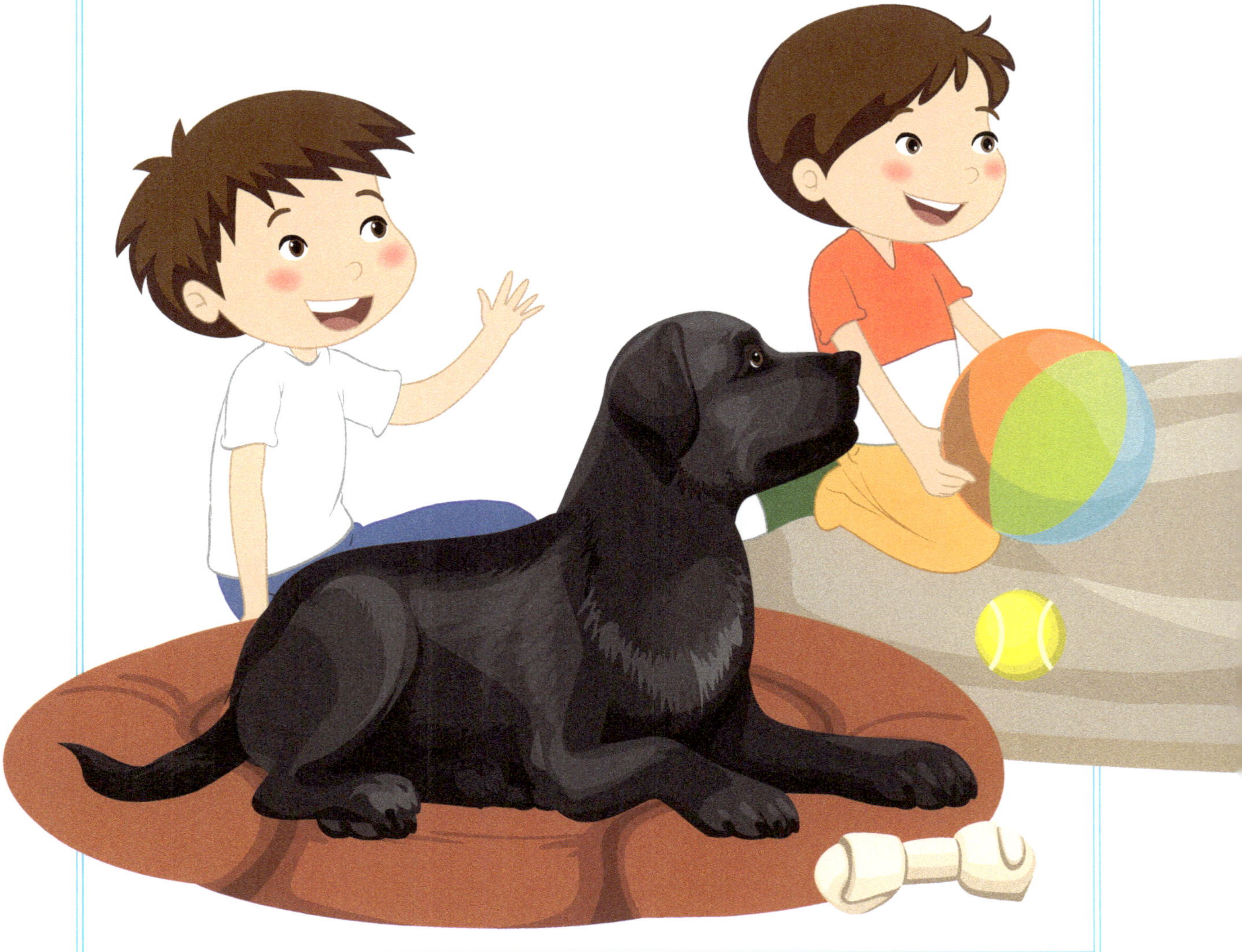

Titus loved to be with us.

So, when Titus got very sick, his veterinarian came to our house. The doctor had an idea. He asked us to sit with Titus and hold him. "Tell Titus he can go ahead and cross the 'Rainbow Bridge,' " the doctor said. "Let him know that you will all be OK without him."

We did.

He did.

When I found Titus's orange collar, I put it under my pillow. On it were two of his black hairs.

Six months after Titus had passed, we decided the time had come to welcome another dog into our family. Together we looked at many different dogs in many different animal shelters. My mom called around to different animal-rescue groups. My dad visited a friend whose black lab had recently given birth to seven black puppies.

Eventually two dogs, a puppy named Cassie and an older dog named Drake, caught our eyes. They became ours and are the best of buddies.

I can still feel Titus with me.
I will always miss him.

But we have pictures of Titus. We have great stories about him.

My mom and dad remind Tanner and me that we should always hold onto our good memories of Titus.

Titus was the best dog.

THE END

About the Author

Cameron, a retired preschool teacher, lives in Oxford, North Carolina, with her husband in her childhood home.

Books are available at
Amazon.com and
BarnesandNoble.com

Other Books by Cameron Pendergraft

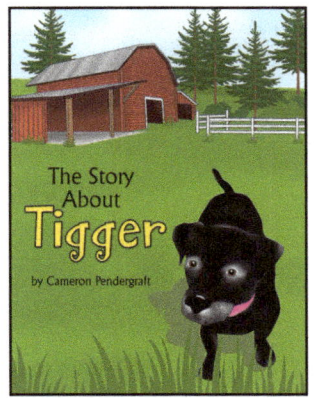

The Story About Tigger

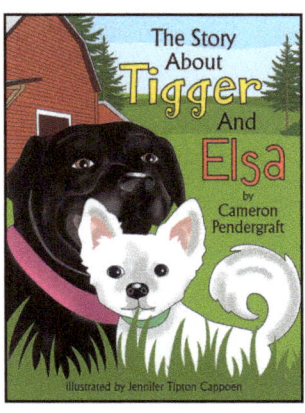

The Story About Tigger And Elsa

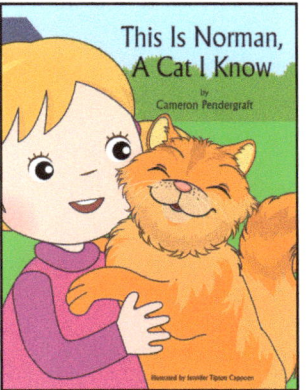

This Is Norman, A Cat I Know

Jack and Rebie

Awake All Night!

www.ingramcontent.com/pod-product-compliance
Lightning Source LLC
Chambersburg PA
CBHW061419090426

42743CB00026B/3496